THE ULTIMATE 10 Sports

OLYMPICS

By Mark Stewart

Gareth Stevens
Publishing

Please visit our web site at www.garethstevens.com.
For a free catalog describing Gareth Stevens Publishing's list of high-quality books, call 1-800-542-2595 (USA)
or 1-800-387-3178 (Canada). Gareth Stevens Publishing's fax: 1-877-542-2596

Library of Congress Cataloging-in-Publication Data
Stewart, Mark, 1960–
    The Olympics / by Mark Stewart.
        p. cm. — (The ultimate 10 sports)
    Includes bibliographical references and index.
    ISBN-10: 0-8368-9160-0 (lib. bdg.)
    ISBN-13: 978-0-8368-9160-7 (lib. bdg.)
    1. Olympics—Juvenile literature. I. Title.
    GV721.5.S76   2009
    796.48—dc22   2008047838

This edition first published in 2009 by
Gareth Stevens Publishing
A Weekly Reader® Company
1 Reader's Digest Road
Pleasantville, NY 10570-7000 USA

Executive Managing Editor: Lisa M. Herrington
Senior Editor: Brian Fitzgerald
Creative Director: Lisa Donovan
Senior Designer: Keith Plechaty
Photo Researcher: Charlene Pinckney
Publisher: Keith Garton

Picture credits
Key: t = top, b = bottom
Cover, title page: (t) CSPA/NewSport/Corbis, (b) Joe Klamar/AFP/Getty Images; pp. 4–5: Al Bello/Getty Images;
p. 7: Focus on Sport/Getty Images; p. 8: (t) Focus on Sport/Getty Images, (b) Bettmann/Corbis; p. 9: AP Images;
p. 11: Bettmann/Corbis; p. 12: (t) © Gerard Rancinan, Jean Guichard/Sygma/Corbis, (b) Bettmann/Corbis;
p. 13: AP Images; p. 15: Presse Sports/US Presswire; p. 16: Bob Donnan/US Presswire; p. 17: Jerry Lai/US Presswire;
p. 19: Billy Stickland/Allsport/Getty Images; p. 20: (t) © William R. Sallaz/NewSport/Corbis, (b) AP Images; p. 21:
William R. Sallaz/NewSport/Corbis; p. 23: Bettmann/Corbis; p. 24: Rolls Press/Popperfoto/Getty Images; p. 25: John
Dominis/Getty Images; p. 27: Jerry Cooke/Corbis; p. 28: (t) AP Images, (b) Bettmann/Corbis; p. 29: Bettmann/Corbis;
p. 31: Peter Dejong/AP Images; p. 32: (t) Peter Dejong/AP Images, (b) Agence Zoom/Getty Images; p. 33: David
Bergman/Corbis; p. 35: Bettmann/Corbis; p. 36: (both) Bettmann/Corbis; p. 37: Walley McNamee/Corbis; p. 39: AFP/
Getty Images; p. 40: (t) Bettmann/Corbis, (b) AP Images; p. 41: Bettmann/Corbis; p. 43: AFP/Getty Images; p. 44:
(t) AFP/Getty Images, (b) Tony Duffy/Getty Images; p. 45: Art Rickerby/Time Life/Getty Images, p. 46: (t) Kirby Lee/
US Presswire, (b) AFP/Getty Images.

Printed in the United States of America

1 2 3 4 5 6 7 8 9 10 09 08

Cover: (top) Michael Phelps races to a gold medal in the 200-meter butterfly; (bottom) Hannah Teter grabs some air at
    the 2006 Olympics.

TABLE OF CONTENTS

Words in the glossary appear in **bold** type
the first time they are used in the text.

THE ULTIMATE 10 Sports

OLYMPICS

Welcome to The Ultimate 10! This exciting series highlights the very best from the world of sports.

Take a front-row seat for some of the most famous moments in Olympics history. You'll meet some of the greatest athletes ever to compete in the Summer and Winter Games. You may never watch sports the same way again!

Every four years, the Olympics celebrate the magic of sports. With so many athletes going for the gold, anything can happen. The unexpected amazing moments are the best part of watching the Olympics. Years later, you will meet people who will say, "Wow, I remember that, too!"

This book tells the stories of 10 "ultimate" Olympic moments. They take place in the air, on the ground, in the water, and on the ice. Each one captures the spirit that makes the Olympics so special.

Michael Phelps prepares to begin a race at the 2008 Games in Beijing, China.

5

#1 The Miracle on Ice

Team USA Shocks the Soviets

February 1980 was a rough time for the United States. Millions of people were out of work. The economy was in bad shape. The Cold War with the Soviet Union had people nervous. The long power struggle between the two countries was at its peak. The American people needed something to shout about. When the Olympics started, no one thought the men's hockey team would give them that chance.

FAST FACTS

MEN'S ICE HOCKEY

OLYMPICS: 1980 Winter Games

LOCATION: Lake Placid, New York, United States

DATE: February 22, 1980

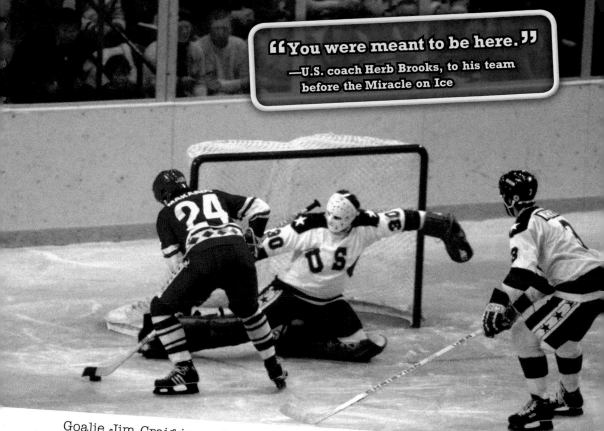

Goalie Jim Craig is ready to make the save on a Soviet shot. Team USA needed a great game from Craig to have a chance.

Cold Warriors

The Soviet hockey team was the best in the world. It was better, some said, than a team of National Hockey League (NHL) All-Stars. Team USA was made up of young, wide-eyed college students. In a warm-up game before the Olympics, the Soviets torched the Americans 10–3.

The Games Begin

U.S. coach Herb Brooks had spent months teaching his young players to believe in themselves. Their confidence showed when they tied Sweden 2–2 and beat Czechoslovakia 7–3. The Swedes and the Czechs were ranked just below the Soviets. The Americans won three more games and moved into the **medal round**. There, Team USA faced the mighty Soviet Union.

U.S. captain Mike Eruzione is surrounded.
He tried all game long to find some open ice.

The Plot Thickens

U.S. fans waved flags and sang patriotic songs at the start of the big game. Almost no one thought Team USA had a chance, however. Goalie Jim Craig made some amazing saves, but the talented Soviets kept up the pressure. They scored three times in the first two periods.

The Americans fought back. Whenever the Soviets scored, Team USA responded with a goal of its own. Mark Johnson scored at the end of the first period to tie the game 2–2. He scored again in the third period to tie the Soviets 3–3.

FOR THE RECORD

The 1980 game was not the first American "miracle" win over the Soviet Union. That came in the 1960 Olympics. The 1960 Soviet team had not lost a game in almost four years. Team USA erased a 2–1 Soviet lead to win 3–2. They went on to beat Czechoslovakia for the gold medal. The last player cut from the U.S. team was Herb Brooks. Twenty years later, he coached Team USA to the gold!

The first "miracle" U.S. team celebrates its victory.

Fantastic Finish

Moments after Johnson's goal, team captain Mike Eruzione fired a shot at the Soviet net. The goalie was blocked by his own teammate and never saw the puck. The shot went in, and Team USA had the lead.

Over the final 10 minutes, the exhausted Americans played tough defense. Craig stopped every shot that came his way. As the last few seconds ticked away, the crowd could not believe what they were seeing. Team USA won 4–3!

Players and fans go wild after Team USA's victory over the Soviets.

DID YOU KNOW?

The victory over the Soviets did not guarantee Team USA a gold medal. They had to beat Finland in their final game. After falling behind 2–1, Team USA made another great comeback to win 4–2.

#2 Jesse Owens, Superman

Race for the Gold

In the 1930s, dictator Adolf Hitler came to power in Germany. He believed that Germany could rule with a race of blond-haired, blue-eyed "supermen." His twisted vision would one day plunge the world into war. The first test of Hitler's theory came at the 1936 Olympics in Berlin. He was counting on the Summer Games to prove that the white race was superior. He didn't count on Jesse Owens.

FAST FACTS

MEN'S TRACK AND FIELD

OLYMPICS: 1936 Summer Games

LOCATION: Berlin, Germany

DATES: August 1–16, 1936

Jesse Owens bursts from the starting block. He was often called "the world's fastest human."

Record Breaker

Owens was the best track-and-field athlete in the United States. As a high school student, he had tied the world record for the 100-yard dash. At a college **meet**, Owens broke three world records and tied a fourth—in less than one hour! One of those records was in the long jump. The mark Owens set that day stood for 25 years.

> **"The battles that count aren't the ones for gold medals."**
> —Jesse Owens

The Games Begin

Owens and his teammates were amazed to hear that the German people expected them to lose. The U.S. track team was the best in the world. Owens alone was expected to win three medals. Hitler claimed that Germans were stronger and smarter than Americans. He promised that the German Olympic team would prove this claim against the "inferior Americans."

The Plot Thickens

On August 3, Owens won the gold medal in the 100-meter dash. He beat out teammate Ralph Metcalfe, another African American. The next day, Owens won gold in a thrilling long-jump battle. He was helped by advice from Germany's Luz Long. The pair became friends during the competition.

On August 5, Owens ran to victory in the 200 meters. His time of 20.7 seconds set a new Olympic record. He now had three gold medals in three tries. Each win earned him bigger cheers from the German crowd.

Jesse Owens glides through the air during his long-jump victory.

Jesse Owens, Ralph Metcalfe, Foy Draper, and Frank Wykoff pose for a photo after the 400-meter relay final.

Fantastic Finish

Owens thought his victory in the 200 meters was his last event. He was surprised to learn that he had been added to the U.S. 400-meter relay team. The runner he replaced, Marty Glickman, was Jewish. Germany was strongly anti-Jewish in the 1930s. Owens knew this and protested, but coach Dean Cromwell gave him no choice.

On August 9, Owens and three teammates tore around the track in 39.8 seconds. They set a world record that stood for 20 years. Owens became the first track athlete to win four gold medals. More important, he proved that Hitler's ideas about race were totally wrong.

DID YOU KNOW?

Owens was never able to make a living as an athlete in the United States. He faced the same racism that many other African Americans did at the time. Even so, he was a proud American. His only regret was that President Franklin D. Roosevelt never congratulated him for his triumph.

#3 Phelps Rules the Pool

Michael Phelps Wins Eight Gold Medals

Michael Phelps stunned the world with six gold medals and two bronzes at the 2004 Olympics. Over the next four years, he put everything he had into preparing for the 2008 Olympics. Phelps wanted to reach the victory stand eight times. That would mean winning the same six races again. In the other two, he would have to turn bronze into gold.

FAST FACTS

MEN'S SWIMMING

OLYMPICS: 2008 Summer Games

LOCATION: Beijing, China

DATES: August 8–24, 2008

> **"You can't put a limit on anything. The more you dream, the farther you get."**
> —Michael Phelps

Michael Phelps competes in the 200-meter butterfly. His long, powerful arms gave him an edge over other swimmers.

Chasing History

No one had ever won eight gold medals in the same Olympics. In 1972, American swimmer Mark Spitz set a record with seven. Phelps could not afford any setbacks if he wanted to break Spitz's record. But in 2007, he slipped on a patch of ice and broke his wrist. He had to train with a kickboard for several weeks. That injury would turn out to be a blessing in disguise.

The Games Begin

In the Olympics, Phelps would swim in five events by himself. He would also swim three as a member of relay teams. His first race was the 400-meter individual **medley**. He had to swim four different strokes—the butterfly, backstroke, breaststroke, and freestyle. Phelps won the race and broke his own world record. Next up was the 400-meter freestyle relay. A record-setting swim by Jason Lezak gave Phelps and his teammates the gold.

Michael Phelps begins the 800-meter freestyle relay for Team USA. The Americans finished far ahead of second-place Russia.

The Plot Thickens

Phelps won his next four medals with ease. He captured gold in the 200-meter freestyle and butterfly. He set new world records in each. He swam the first leg of the 800-meter freestyle relay, helping the U.S. team beat Russia by five seconds. He then set another world record in the 200-meter individual medley. Phelps had six gold medals with two races to go.

FOR THE RECORD

Michael Phelps has won more gold medals than any other Olympian.

ATHLETE	SPORT	GOLD MEDALS	TOTAL MEDALS*
Michael Phelps	Swimming	14	16
Larissa Latynina	Gymnastics	9	18
Paavo Nurmi	Running	9	12
Mark Spitz	Swimming	9	11
Carl Lewis	Track and Field	9	10

* Includes silver and bronze medals

Yeah! Michael Phelps learns that he has won the 100-meter butterfly by only 0.01 second.

Fantastic Finish

In swimming, the difference between first place and second place can be the blink of an eye. In the 100-meter butterfly, Phelps fell behind Milorad Cavic. As they neared the wall, Phelps used his incredible leg strength to pull closer. His training with the kickboard paid off. He touched the wall one one-hundredth of a second before Cavic to win the race.

One day later, Phelps and his teammates won the 400-meter medley relay in record time. It was his record-setting eighth gold medal.

DID YOU KNOW?

How great was Michael Phelps at the 2008 Olympics? Only eight countries won more gold medals than he did. He won as many golds as Italy and one fewer than Japan.

#4 The Miracle on the Mat

Rulon Gardner Stuns the Wrestling World

Alexander Karelin was like the Tiger Woods or Michael Jordan of Greco-Roman wrestling. The Russian strongman had gone 13 years without losing a match. He looked to extend his streak against American Rulon Gardner at the 2000 Olympics. Did goofy, good-natured Gardner stand a chance against Karelin? The experts chuckled at the thought. Guess who had the last laugh.

FAST FACTS

MEN'S 130 KG WRESTLING

OLYMPICS: 2000 Summer Games

LOCATION: Sydney, Australia

DATE: September 27, 2000

Rulon Gardner (right) is in trouble early in his match with Alexander Karelin. Karelin's great strength made him almost unbeatable.

Strong Man

Karelin had won Olympic gold medals in 1988, 1992, and 1996. When the 2000 Olympics began, everyone expected him to win again. Karelin's favorite move was the reverse body lift. Karelin would grab his opponent around the waist. The Russian would then use his incredible strength to lift his opponent over his head and slam him to the mat.

The Games Begin

Gardner was strong, too. He built up his strength and stamina working on his family's farm in Wyoming. But Karelin's body seemed to be chiseled out of stone. Gardner looked more like a giant helping of mashed potatoes. Standing next to Karelin before their gold-medal match, the farm boy did not appear to have a chance.

Greco-Roman wrestlers are not allowed to attack below the waist. Wrestlers score points by picking up an opponent and throwing him to the mat. That is called a **takedown**. Points can be scored in other ways, such as gaining an advantage over an opponent from a defensive position. That is called a **reversal**. When Gardner met Karelin, points also were awarded for an escape.

Rulon Gardner tries to prevent Alexander Karelin from getting underneath him.

Alexander Karelin loses his grip on his young opponent.

The Plot Thickens

All Karelin needed to do was get a good grip on Gardner. Then he could toss him, flip him, or pick him up and drop him on his head. But no matter what the Russian tried, Gardner slithered out of his grasp. Karelin started to lift him a couple of times, but he could not get a good grip on Gardner. After the first three-minute round, neither wrestler had scored a point.

Fantastic Finish

At the start of the second round, Karelin made an error. He had Gardner in a hold that was nearly impossible to break. For some reason, Karelin released his opponent. That gave Gardner a point for an escape. The referee was so surprised that he did not give Gardner the point at first. No one had scored on Karelin since 1994!

With a 1–0 lead, Gardner just needed to survive. After three periods, the exhausted Gardner was declared the winner. He did a cartwheel as Karelin quietly disappeared under the stands.

> **"I kept saying, 'I think I can. I think I can.' But it wasn't until it was over that I knew I could."**
> —Rulon Gardner

Rulon Gardner can't believe he is wearing a gold medal. Neither could the rest of the wrestling world!

DID YOU KNOW?

After winning his match against Karelin, Gardner continued to beat the odds. In 2002, he was stranded in the wilderness during a snowmobile trip. He lost a toe to frostbite. In 2004, he was hit by a car. In 2007, his plane crashed into a lake. Each time, Gardner lived to see another day.

#5 The Longest Jump

Bob Beamon Defies Gravity

If people were meant to fly, they'd have wings. Bob Beamon probably does not believe that old saying. For one incredible moment, Beamon broke free of the grip of gravity. At the 1968 Olympics, he jumped higher and farther than any person in history. In doing so, Beamon showed the power of the Olympics to bring out the very best in athletes.

FAST FACTS

MEN'S LONG JUMP

OLYMPICS: 1968 Summer Games

LOCATION: Mexico City, Mexico

DATE: October 18, 1968

"I was ready. I felt very peaceful and calm. My body was never more relaxed."

—Bob Beamon, on his record-breaking jump

Olympic officials watch as Bob Beamon jumps his way into history.

Leap of Faith

Beamon arrived at the 1968 Olympics without a coach. Earlier that year, he had refused to compete against a school that he believed had racist policies. His college coach suspended him from the team. Beamon was still the favorite in Mexico City. He had won 22 of 23 meets before the Games. Another long jumper, Ralph Boston, agreed to help Beamon. At the time, Boston shared the world record of 27 feet 4¾ inches (8.35 meters).

Game On

In the qualifying round, Beamon almost **fouled** out of the competition. He stepped over the takeoff line twice. Boston told him to mark off a spot a foot in front of the line. That way, he would take off well in front of it. Beamon's third jump was long enough to move him into the medal round.

Bob Beamon shows the form that would earn him a new world record.

The Plot Thickens

Beamon was one of 17 jumpers competing for the gold. The weather was poor. A slight drizzle made the track slippery. The first three jumpers fouled. Beamon jumped fourth. As Beamon sprinted down the track, he remembered his fouls in the earlier round. With each step, he told himself, "Don't foul, don't foul." He hit the takeoff board perfectly and launched into the air.

FOR THE RECORD

Bob Beamon's record stood for more than two decades. American long jumper Mike Powell broke it in 1991. Here are the top five jumps in history, through 2008:

ATHLETE	COUNTRY	YEAR	DISTANCE
Mike Powell	United States	1991	29 ft. 4½ in. (8.95 m)
Bob Beamon	United States	1968	29 ft. 2½ in. (8.90 m)
Carl Lewis	United States	1991	29 ft. 1¼ in. (8.87 m)
Robert Emmiyan	Soviet Union	1987	29 ft. 1 in. (8.86 m)
Larry Myricks	United States	1988	28 ft. 8¼ in. (8.74 m)

Fantastic Finish

Beamon almost seemed to "run" through the air—and just kept going and going. He hit the sandpit and bounced right up. The crowd erupted. They knew Beamon had landed a great jump. But no one realized just how great it was.

The distance was too long for the measuring device to record. Officials had to use an old-fashioned tape measure. The scoreboard flashed 8.90 meters. Beamon was unfamiliar with the metric system. Finally, he learned that he had jumped 29 feet 2½ inches. That broke the world record by nearly 2 feet! Beamon collapsed when he realized what he had done.

Teammates Ralph Boston and Charlie Mays hold Bob Beamon after he learns that he has broken the world record.

> **❝Compared to this jump, we are as children.❞**
>
> —Soviet long jumper
> Igor Ter-Ovanesyan

After his record jump, Beamon still had two more attempts. His second jump was almost 3 feet shorter than his first. He decided to stop. The silver medal winner did not come within 2 feet of Beamon's record. Beamon himself never came close to matching his amazing jump.

#6 Rise and Shine

Wilma Rudolph Wins Triple Gold

There is a lot pressure to win when you're called "the world's fastest woman." Wilma Rudolph carried that title into the 1960 Olympics. But she was feeling almost no pressure at all. For Rudolph, pressure was growing up poor in a family with 22 children. Pressure was struggling through childhood with a brace on one leg. Pressure was something the other runners felt when they faced off against Rudolph.

FAST FACTS

WOMEN'S TRACK AND FIELD

OLYMPICS: 1960 Summer Games

LOCATION: Rome, Italy

DATES: August 25–September 11, 1960

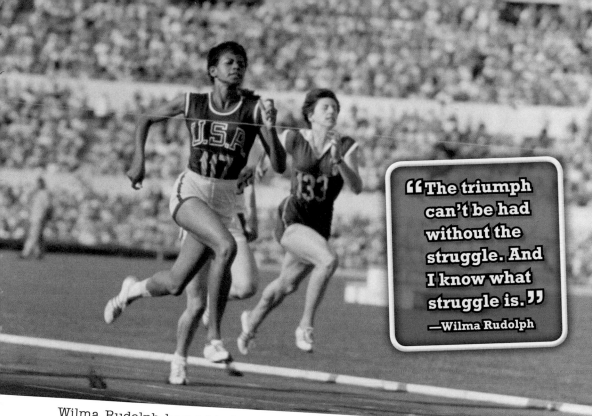

> **"The triumph can't be had without the struggle. And I know what struggle is."**
> —Wilma Rudolph

Wilma Rudolph has a big lead as she nears the finish line. She hoped to win three gold medals in 1960.

Stand and Deliver

As a child, Wilma Rudolph had polio, scarlet fever, and double pneumonia. For a time, she could not use her left leg. Family members took turns rubbing her leg to build strength. By age 11, she could finally walk without special shoes or braces. By age 14, she was competing in races. Two years later, she was running in the 1956 Olympics!

The Games Begin

In 1960, Rudolph was a member of the Tennessee State University Tigerbelles. They were the top college track team. She was also the star of the U.S. Olympic track-and-field squad. At the Olympics, Rudolph planned to run in three events—the 100 meters, 200 meters, and 400-meter relay. Four years earlier, Betty Cuthbert of Australia had set a record by winning gold in all three.

FOR THE RECORD

Wilma Rudolph was not the only Olympian to overcome physical challenges. In 1990, doctors told U.S. sprinter Gail Devers (right) that she had Graves disease. The illness affected her muscles and her eyes. She underwent radiation treatment. She became so weak that she could barely walk. Devers did not give up. She regained her strength and got back into shape. She went on to win gold in the 100 meters in 1992 and 1996.

The Plot Thickens

Rudolph was one of the most relaxed athletes anyone had ever seen. She actually fell asleep before one of her races and then woke up to win easily. Rudolph won her first gold medal in the 100 meters. She broke the tape in 11 seconds. On her way to the 200-meter final, Rudolph smashed the Olympic record in that event. She easily won her second gold.

Wilma Rudolph breaks the tape as she wins another race.

The Tigerbelles pose for a photo. Wilma Rudolph is on the left, next to Lucinda Williams, Barbara Jones, and Martha Hudson.

Fantastic Finish

In the 400-meter relay, Rudolph went for her third gold medal. All four runners were members of the Tigerbelles. Martha Hudson, Lucinda Williams, and Barbara Jones opened a good lead on the German team. But Jones and Rudolph lost the lead when they had a sloppy exchange of the **baton**. Rudolph quickly recovered. She blew past Jutta Heine to win by three-tenths of a second. The incredible Rudolph had her third gold medal.

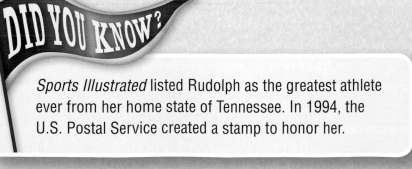

DID YOU KNOW?

Sports Illustrated listed Rudolph as the greatest athlete ever from her home state of Tennessee. In 1994, the U.S. Postal Service created a stamp to honor her.

#7 The Golden Tomato

Shaun White Wins a Snowboarding Gold

In the world of extreme sports, Shaun White was a superstar. Fans called the talented redhead "the Flying Tomato." It was hard to find a teenager who didn't know his name. To most older sports fans, however, White was a mystery. They considered his event, snowboarding, a sideshow at the Olympics. All that changed at the 2006 Games in Turin, Italy.

FAST FACTS

MEN'S SNOWBOARDING HALF-PIPE

OLYMPICS: 2006 Winter Games

LOCATION: Turin, Italy

DATE: February 12, 2006

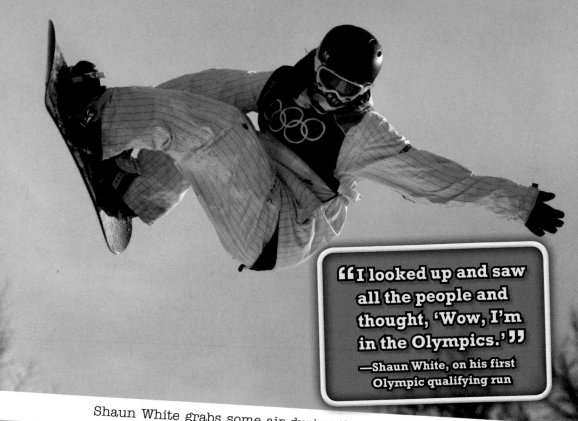

Shaun White grabs some air during the 2006 Olympics.

Pipe Dreams

Snowboarding had become an Olympic sport in 1998. But the sport was not truly in the spotlight in the Olympics until 2006. The biggest event was the **half-pipe**, an acrobatic competition with roots in skateboarding. It was no surprise that White was the king of the half-pipe. He started out as a champion skateboarder. His specialty was the 1080—three complete 360-degree midair spins. He planned to mix these in with longer, higher, slower-spinning jumps.

The Games Begin

White was confident that he would win a gold medal. He had beaten all the top snowboarders in the **X Games**. But something was different in Turin. White and the other snowboarders felt the added pressure of the Olympics. He started to tense up. On his first qualifying run, he fell.

The Plot Thickens

Only the top six snowboarders would make the finals. White was seventh with one run left. He headed down the mountain with heavy metal music pounding out of speakers around the course. White played it safe—he did not try a 1080. But he landed all of his jumps perfectly. White scored 45.3 out of 50 possible points and moved on to the finals.

This is what "playing it safe" looks like when your name is Shaun White!

FOR THE RECORD

Shaun White was not the only snowboarding star at the Olympics. Another American, Hannah Teter, won the women's half-pipe. Teter had the fifth-highest score in the qualifying round. In the finals, she posted the two highest scores of the day to freeze out the competition. Her teammate Gretchen Bleiler won the silver.

Hannah Teter shows her colors after winning the gold.

Fantastic Finish

White was even better in the finals. On his first run, he landed a McTwist—an upside-down 540-degree spin. Next, he nailed back-to-back 1080s. He finished off with perfect back-to-back 900s. White's score was 46.8. No one else was able to top his score. The 19-year-old redhead had won the gold medal. When White returned to the United States, sports fans from ages 7 to 70 mobbed him wherever he went. He was unknown no more!

All right! Shaun White sees his score of 46.8.

" I didn't know if I would get the gold, I just knew I wanted it. "
—Shaun White

DID YOU KNOW?

Few athletes are as laid-back as White. But after he received his gold medal, the power of the Olympics caught him by surprise. As the national anthem played, White welled up with tears.

#8 Picture Perfect

Nadia Comaneci
Earns Seven 10s

Before the 1976 Olympics, everyone was talking about Nadia Comaneci. She had earned scores of 10 points during major international meets. In other words, the 14-year-old from Romania had been perfect. Could she do it in the Olympics? The competition and judges would be tougher than any she had ever faced. Millions of fans tuned in to find out.

FAST FACTS

WOMEN'S GYMNASTICS
OLYMPICS: 1976 Summer Games
LOCATION: Montreal, Canada
DATES: July 17–August 1, 1976

Tiny Teens

During the 1950s and 1960s, women's gymnastics was ruled by big, strong, mature athletes. During the 1972 Olympics, fans fell in love with young, bubbly Olga Korbut of the Soviet Union. She was smaller than the other gymnasts, but her moves were daring and dangerous. In 1976, all eyes were on Comaneci. She stood 4 feet 11 inches and weighed just 86 pounds.

The Games Begin

During the team competition, Comaneci finished her routine on the **uneven bars** without making a mistake. Fans were amazed when they looked at the scoreboard. It showed 1.00. Comaneci had actually received a score of 10, but the scoreboard did not go that high! She scored another 10 on the balance beam. Hers were the first perfect scores awarded in an Olympics.

Nadia Comaneci tries a daring move on the balance beam.

> **❝ Her precision and daring in gymnastics have never been seen before in an Olympics. ❞**
> —Sportswriter Frank DeFord

FOR THE RECORD

Comaneci was not the only gymnast to receive perfect scores during the 1976 Olympics. Nelli Kim of the Soviet Union (right) earned 10s for her **vault** and floor exercise. She won gold medals in both events. Kim also scored a 10 in the vault during the all-around competition. Comaneci and Kim faced off again at the 1980 Olympics. They tied for a gold medal in the floor exercise.

The Plot Thickens

Comaneci's perfection helped the Romanian team win a silver medal. Next, she competed for individual medals. Comaneci was fearless. She tried dangerous moves without blinking an eye. On the balance beam, she wowed the judges with precise flips and handstands. Crowds watched with open mouths as she scored more 10s. She won gold medals in the uneven bars and balance beam. She also captured a bronze in the floor exercise.

Nadia Comaneci goes for a perfect 10 on the balance beam.

Fantastic Finish

Comaneci was brilliant in the all-around competition. The all-around included four events: the vault, uneven bars, balance beam, and floor exercise. Comaneci scored two more 10s, on the beam and bars. She did well enough in the other two events to capture the gold medal, ahead of Nelli Kim. Comaneci finished with three golds, one silver, one bronze—and seven perfect 10s.

Nadia Comaneci waves to the crowd after winning one of her three gold medals.

DID YOU KNOW?

If Comaneci were competing today, the results would be very different. First, 14-year-olds can no longer take part in the Olympics. The minimum age is 16. Also, the scoring in gymnastics has changed. Since 2006, gymnasts no longer receive perfect 10s.

#9 Fab Five

Eric Heiden
Dominates the Ice

In the weeks before the 1980 Winter Olympics, speed skater Eric Heiden was the most talked-about athlete in the United States. Heiden was more than just the country's best hope for a gold medal. There were five speed-skating events in Lake Placid. Heiden had a chance to win them all. No skater had ever done that before. But then, Heiden was like no other skater.

FAST FACTS

MEN'S SPEED SKATING

OLYMPICS: 1980 Winter Games

LOCATION: Lake Placid, New York, United States

DATES: February 14–23, 1980

"I thought I could win maybe one or two medals. But five? I thought it was out of the question."
—Eric Heiden

Eric Heiden leans into a turn during the 1980 Olympics. He used his thick, powerful legs to generate incredible speed.

Unknown at Home

Speed skating was an unknown sport in the United States during the 1970s. Most sports fans had no idea who Heiden was until just before the 1980 Olympics. As they learned more about him, they became excited. Heiden had a slim, sleek upper body. Each of his powerful thighs was almost as big as his waist. He was a speed-skating monster!

The Games Begin

The longest speed-skating event in the Olympics is 10,000 meters—more than 6 miles. The shortest is 500 meters. The three other distances are 1,000, 1,500, and 5,000 meters. Winning the longer races takes great strength and stamina. Winning the shorter ones takes explosive power. Before Heiden came along, many experts thought it was impossible for one skater to have all of these qualities.

The Plot Thickens

The wildest race for Heiden was his first, the 500 meters. He skated against Yevgeny Kulikov, the world record holder. They were even until the final turn, when Kulikov slipped ever so slightly. Heiden crossed the line three-tenths of a second ahead of him. It was one of the most exciting races anyone could remember.

As expected, Heiden won the 5,000 meters and the 1,000 meters easily. In the 1,500 meters, he nearly fell when his skate hit a crack in the ice. But Heiden kept his balance and went on to win. He had now won four gold medals and set Olympic records in each race.

Eric Heiden strains for the finish line in the 500 meters.

FOR THE RECORD

The day before his final race, Heiden watched the U.S. hockey team stun the Soviet Union in the Miracle on Ice. His friends Bob Suter and Mark Johnson were on the team. As a boy, Heiden had been a hockey player, too. He was so excited by the U.S. victory that he could not sleep before his 10,000-meter race!

Mark Johnson scores the first of his two goals against the Soviets.

Fantastic Finish

Heiden lined up for the start of his final race, the 10,000 meters. He was seeking his fifth gold medal in nine days. Heiden skated with great poise and power. During the race, the crowd stood and cheered, "Eric! Eric! Eric!" Heiden shattered the world record by an amazing six seconds. He did what many had thought was impossible. He became the first athlete to win five individual gold medals in one Olympics.

Eric Heiden shows off his record five gold medals. He later quit skating to become a doctor.

"Gold, silver, and bronze isn't special. It's giving 100 percent and knowing you've done the best you can."

—Eric Heiden

DID YOU KNOW?

Heiden did not like being an American sports celebrity. He soon retired from skating and became a professional cyclist. He competed in the 1986 **Tour de France**. Later, Heiden became a doctor. He was the team doctor for the U.S. speed-skating team at the 2006 Olympics.

#10 Queen of the Ice

Peggy Fleming's Olympic Miracle

In 1961, a plane crash killed the entire U.S. figure skating team. That made 12-year-old Peggy Fleming the last great hope for U.S. skating in the 1960s. Fleming studied under a new coach and wore costumes sewn by her mother. She blossomed into a different kind of skater—and changed the face of her sport.

FAST FACTS

WOMEN'S FIGURE SKATING

OLYMPICS: 1968 Winter Games

LOCATION: Grenoble, France

DATES: February 6–18, 1968

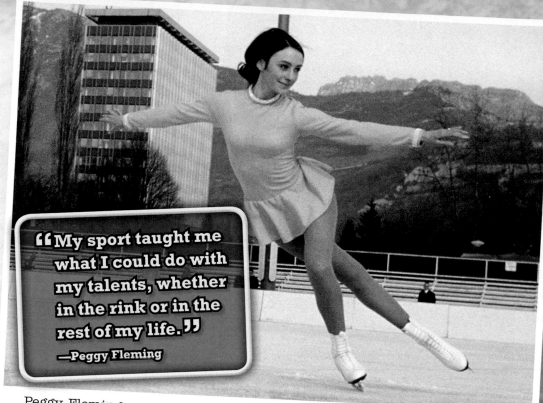

> ❝My sport taught me what I could do with my talents, whether in the rink or in the rest of my life.❞
> —Peggy Fleming

Peggy Fleming practices for her gold-medal performance. She brought something magical to her sport.

Ice Princess

Fleming's new coach was Carlo Fassi. Both of them believed that figure skaters did not bring out the full beauty of the sport. The pair worked together to create a new skating style. It was a mix of perfect technique, amazing athletic skill, and artistic beauty. Fleming did not simply skate to the music she chose. Every move she made expressed the mood of the song. No one else in the world skated like her. By 1966, no one in the world could beat her.

The Games Begin

The 1968 Olympics were the first Winter Games broadcast in color. People who had never watched figure skating were glued to their TVs. Americans did not have much else to cheer about. No other U.S. team or athlete was able to win a gold medal.

The Plot Thickens

Fleming skated her technical routine on the first day. The judges scored each skater on how precisely she completed certain moves. Fleming's scores were so high that it was almost impossible for anyone to catch her. The second half of the competition was the free-skate program. There, skaters would show off all their talents in a routine set to music. Fleming needed only to play it safe to win the gold medal.

Judges watch Peggy Fleming skate during her technical program.

FOR THE RECORD

All of the U.S. team's coaches died in the 1961 tragedy. Carlo Fassi had the difficult job of making the team great again. After the 1968 Olympics, he became the sport's most famous coach. His top student was Dorothy Hamill. She won a gold medal at the 1976 Olympics. Like Peggy Fleming, Hamill inspired countless young skaters. She also set a fashion trend. Thousands of women copied her hairstyle!

Dorothy Hamill inspired thousands of girls to try figure skating.

Fantastic Finish

Fleming held back nothing in the free skate. She glided across the ice in a stunning light-green dress. Her jumps and spins showed her athletic ability. Her grace and artistry set her apart from the other skaters. Fleming won the gold medal by an amazing 88 points.

Young skaters who saw Fleming that day realized that their sport had reached a new level. Her performance marked the beginning of a new era in figure skating.

Peggy Fleming performs her free skate. Her artistry won over many new skating fans.

> **"Her energy got the train of U.S. figure skating moving again. Once it got rolling, nothing has stopped it since."**
>
> —U.S. skating coach Linda Leaver, on Peggy Fleming

DID YOU KNOW?

Fleming became one of the most beloved celebrities in the United States. She helped TV viewers understand and appreciate figure skating as a performer and later as a broadcaster. She also became an important voice for physical fitness and cancer awareness.

Honorable Mentions

Lightning Bolt

2008 Summer Olympics
Beijing, China

Tall runners do not make good sprinters. They take too long to get up to full speed. No one told that to 6-foot 5-inch Usain Bolt. He dominated the 2008 Olympics like no sprinter had before. The Jamaican star easily won gold in the 100 meters, 200 meters, and 400-meter relay. He became the first sprinter to set world records in all three events in one Olympics.

Seoul Sister

1988 Summer Olympics
Seoul, South Korea

Most people knew Florence Griffith Joyner by her nickname, "Flo-Jo." She brought glamour and style to track and field. At the 1988 Olympics, Flo-Jo won four sprinting medals. She won the 100 meters and set a world record in the 200 meters. She was also a member of the gold-medal 400-meter relay team.

Glossary

baton: the object passed between runners during a running relay

fouled: stepped over the takeoff line. When a long jumper fouls, the jump does not count.

half-pipe: a snowboarding course that is shaped like the letter U or like a pipe cut in half

medal round: the "finals" of Olympic competition, when the gold, silver, and bronze medalists are determined

medley: a swimming race that includes four different strokes—backstroke, breaststroke, butterfly, and freestyle

meet: an athletic competition between two or more teams, most often in swimming or track and field

reversal: a wrestling move in which a wrestler in a defensive position gains an advantage over an opponent

takedown: a wrestling move in which one wrestler throws the other to the mat

Tour de France: the most famous bicycle race in the world. The Tour de France takes place each July.

uneven bars: a piece of equipment that is part of gymnastics events. The bars are parallel but set at different heights.

vault: a gymnastics event in which athletes spring into the air and perform twists and spins before landing

X Games: an annual competition of extreme sports created by the TV network ESPN

For More Information

Books

Ballheimer, David, and Chris Oxlade. *Olympics.* DK Eyewitness Books. New York: DK Children, 2005.

Christopher, Matt. *The Olympics: Legendary Sports Events.* New York: Little, Brown, 2008.

Goldish, Meish. *Michael Phelps: Anything Is Possible!* Defining Moments. New York: Bearport Publishing, 2009.

Israel, Elaine. *Jesse Owens: Running Into History.* Time for Kids Biographies. New York: Collins, 2006.

Web Sites

Index

About the Author

Mark Stewart is the "ultimate" sports author. He has published more than 100 sports biographies and histories, but this is his first book strictly on the Olympics. Mark has written books about several Olympic gold medalists, including LeBron James, Lisa Leslie, and Mia Hamm. During the 1990s, Mark worked with Florence Griffith Joyner on her authorized biography.